TRUE ADVENTURES

ANNE ADENEY

Copyright © Anne Adeney 2003
First published 2003

Cover design: Paul Airy
Cover illustration: Christopher Rothero

Scripture Union, 207–209 Queensway, Bletchley,
Milton Keynes, MK2 2EB, England.
Email: info@scriptureunion.org.uk
Website: www.scriptureunion.org.uk

ISBN 1 85999 269 2

British Library Cataloguing-in-Publication Data.
A catalogue record of this book is available from the
British Library.

Printed and bound in Great Britain by Creative Print and
Design (Wales) Ebbw Vale.

Scripture Union is an international Christian charity
working with churches in more than 130 countries,
providing resources to bring the good news about Jesus
Christ to children, young people and families and to
encourage them to develop spiritually through the Bible
and prayer.

As well as our network of volunteers, staff and
associates who run holidays, church-based events and
school Christian groups, we produce a wide range of
publications and support those who use our resources
through training programmes.

To my four wonderful daughters:
Jenny, Libby, Katy and Megan,
with much love.

Contents

Chapter One

From master to slave

North West England, AD *399*

"Help! Save me!"

Succat rolled over and pulled the blanket more tightly round his shoulders. If it was the slaves making that awful noise he'd have them whipped! His father, Calpurnius, was the local Roman ruler. He had been entertaining important people last night. They had all dined late, on roast boar and wine, and Succat was not ready to get up yet. He lazily opened one eye. Dawn was just beginning to paint the skies with a rosy glow. It was far too early! Those slaves were in big trouble! The screams came again.

"Father, help me! Mother! Save me!"

Succat sat up with a start. That was no slave. That was the voice of his sister, Lupita! He leapt out of bed and pulled on his short tunic. He raced out of his room, the mosaic tiles cold under his bare feet. A red-bearded giant was dragging Lupita through the door.

"Help me, Succat!" she screamed.

Pirates! Irish pirates! "Let her go!" Succat yelled.

He hurled himself at the heavily built man. He kicked and pounded at him with his fists. The burly man pushed him aside as if he were a fly. The pirate gathered Lupita up under his huge arm and headed down towards the shore. Succat looked around wildly. Where were Father and Mother? Where were the slaves?

Running out of the villa, he found his questions horribly answered. The rosy glow he had seen in the sky was not dawn, but the burning roofs of the houses in the nearby village of Bannavem Taberniae. All around him people were being dragged or carried down to the shore by gigantic shaggy figures with drawn and blood stained swords.

Suddenly he was lifted into the air and flung over a wide shoulder as easily as if he were a baby and not a fourteen-year-old boy. Succat felt sick as the smell of the pirate filled his nostrils. He was used to having a hot bath every day, followed by a massage with aromatic oils by his body slave. This monster smelt as if he'd never had a bath in his life!

Down on the shore the raider threw Succat onto the ground and prodded him to his feet with his sword. The sharp shingle cut into his bare feet. The pain was only dulled by the icy cold of the sea water as he and a group of others were herded out to a large reed boat. The wild Irish pirate leapt in after them, roaring with triumph at the successful raid.

Cowering on the bottom of the curach, Succat could see many of these boats. The pirates were driving dozens of local people into them. The air was filled with the smell of smoke and blood and the sound of blood-curdling screams. The pirates swiftly set sail and soon gut-wrenching seasickness added to Succat's misery.

"What will become of us?" whimpered a girl.

"Sold as slaves!" muttered a man.

"They're all pagans in Ireland!" wailed one of the women. "They know nothing of our Christian God!"

They had to endure a long voyage in the open boat and constant soaking from the icy waves. Exhaustion and terror quietened the captives. The roar of delight from the ragged Irish pirate and the slap of the cold grey waves against the side of the curach were the only sounds to be heard when they eventually reached the coast of Ireland.

They landed on the coast of County Antrim, where the Britons were tied together like animals and marched to the market place. Here the pirate ripped off Succat's fine wool tunic and threw him a dirty piece of sacking to wear in its place. Succat had never smelt anything so revolting and the thought of wearing it filled him with disgust. He was a rich man's son and used to the best of everything. But anything was better than appearing naked before the world. He took the foul stuff and reluctantly tied it round his body.

The sale of the captured Britons in the market place was even more humiliating. It was bad enough being like an animal waiting to be sold. But nobody wanted to buy him! Lupita was nowhere to be seen. His companions were mostly farming folk from the village and a few slaves from his father's villa. They were all strong and would make good slaves for the Irishmen. But Succat was still a small boy, with no muscles and soft white skin.

"What a skinny runt!"

"He couldn't lift a peat turf to save his life!"

"Those soft hands have never seen a day's work!"

"You might as well buy a baby girl as the likes of him!"

Succat couldn't understand the strange language of the rough Irish farmers, but their meaning was all too clear as they prodded and laughed at him.

At last a tall figure, wearing a long sheepskin cloak, came into the market place. He offered to buy Succat, but only at a bargain price. This was an Irish chieftain called Míleac mac Boin. He was a hard, cruel man, one of Ireland's powerful Druids.

The rich young Roman citizen was now put to work as a slave. Instead of wild boar and larks' tongues, he ate hard black bread and occasionally some rancid cheese or nearly rotten meat. He cleaned out Míleac's stables. He picked up stones from the fields until his back was on fire with pain. But eventually Míleac made him a shepherd boy.

Life out on Slemish Mountain was vastly different from his life as the son of a wealthy ruler. There were no feasts and entertainments. He no longer had lessons in Latin and swordsmanship. For a long time Succat was miserable and in despair.

Then one day he saw three figures coming up the mountainside. He recognised them as the son and daughters of Míleac. The smaller girl came over and shyly offered him a soft barley cake. Succat took it and devoured it in three bites. The girl giggled and pointed to herself.

"Enda!" she said. She pointed to her sister and said, "Maev!"

The boy thumped himself on the chest and said,

"Art!" Then he prodded Succat and looked questioningly at him.

Succat announced his name proudly and then was most put out when the other children burst out laughing at this strange name. Art shook his head violently.

"That's a terrible name!" he said to his sisters. "Let's call him Patrick!"

So Patrick he became. As he became more used to the hard work and cold conditions he felt more at peace with his work. He began to enjoy the peaceful life on the mountainside with the sheep. Míleac's children often came up to play with him and bring him food.

They played the sort of games that children have always played, running and chasing and climbing trees. Patrick was a very clever boy and soon picked up the Irish language. He learnt that Art's name meant stone and also bear, and that bears were sacred here. Little Enda's name meant bird and Maev was the name of a famous queen. But what the children of Míleac liked most was to hear stories about Patrick's life when he was a boy called Succat, in Roman Britain.

Patrick spent many hours alone with his sheep. At first these were hours when he thought about home constantly. He remembered, with bitter regret, how he'd often missed family prayers to go fishing with his friends. He had been bored by Christian worship and tried to avoid it whenever he could, although his father was a deacon and his grandfather a priest. He had also done bad things. But a change came over Patrick in the quiet of the hills. As he tended his sheep he thought about

Jesus, the Good Shepherd. He remembered the words that his mother, Concessa, used to read to him from the Psalms. The strong words surrounded him like a warm blanket. He grew closer to God, praying to him and listening to him. Sometimes he said up to a hundred prayers in a day, and as many at night. During his prayer times he never felt the cold wind, the icy rain or the blinding snow.

Once he dreamed that he was imprisoned under a huge stone that had fallen from a wall. Suddenly he felt the stone being lifted and God's hands putting it back on the wall.

"You are like this stone, Patrick," said God. "For a while you fell off my wall and lay in the mud. But I've put you back now. I've forgiven you for the bad things you've done. In future you will do important work for me."

But Patrick had to learn patience, because it was a long time before God called him to this work. Six years passed and Patrick became a strong young man. One night the snow was falling thickly and he could hear wolves howling in the distance. So Patrick gathered all his sheep into the stone sheepfold and curled up beside their warm bodies to sleep. He had another dream in which he heard a voice calling to him.

"Look! Your ship is ready! Soon you will be home with your own people!"

Patrick knew that this was a message from God. He walked for 200 miles to find that ship and, after many adventures, he returned home. His parents were overjoyed to see him.

After some years Patrick heard the people of Ireland calling out to him in another dream. They called him, "Holy boy," and begged him to return to Ireland. Then Patrick realised what job God had in mind for him. He went to study with his uncle, St Martin of Tours, in France and became a priest. Eventually Patrick was made a bishop and went to Ireland to preach Christianity in AD 433.

Fact file 1 file 2

- Patrick was born in Scotland in AD 385.

- His name was Maewyn Succat, but he officially took the name of Patrick when he became a priest.

- His father, Calpurnius, was a powerful Roman ruler.

- Patrick was captured by Irish pirates in AD 399 and sold into slavery.

- Six years later he escaped, after a dream when God told him to leave Ireland by ship. He eventually returned home to his parents. In another dream the people of Ireland begged him to return.

- He returned to his master to pay back the money with which Míleac had bought him. But the chieftain thought the now powerful missionary was coming to seek revenge. His pride could not endure defeat by his former slave and he put all his belongings onto a fire and threw himself on it.

Fact | Fact file 2

- Míleac's three children were overjoyed to see Patrick and were baptised. We don't know their real names, but we know that the son became a priest and the daughters became nuns and founded a convent.

- He preached all over Ireland for 40 years, worked many miracles and converted many thousands.

- The conversion of Ireland was not easy. Patrick endured much suffering and was captured 12 times.

- Patrick used a three-leafed shamrock to explain the Trinity and it has since been used as the national emblem of Ireland.

- It is said that Patrick banished all snakes from Ireland. But the truth is that there were no snakes in Ireland after the Ice Age. This is probably a word picture of him driving the wickedness of the pagans out of Ireland.

- Patrick died in AD 461, on 17 March, which is dedicated to him as Saint Patrick's Day.

Chapter Two

The monk and the monster

Scotland, AD *565*

"Open this door in the name of the Lord!" roared Columba, pounding on the great wooden door with his stout staff.

Kieran shivered with fear. On the other side of the vast door were King Brude and all his men. Surely it was madness for three monks and one small boy to demand entrance to the royal home of the King of the Picts himself! He longed to run away and find somewhere safe to hide. Kieran was very scared of the pagan tribes of Scotland that Columba had been sent to convert to Christianity.

"Get away from here, you mad Irishmen!" came an even louder bellow from inside the strong stockade. "We've heard about you and your crazy stories, and King Brude wants nothing to do with you! Now, be off, or you'll be moving out on the ends of our swords!"

There was a loud crash, as the strong iron bolts on the gates were slammed into place. Kieran breathed a sigh of relief and turned to walk away.

"Wait!" ordered Columba. "We have not yet done what we came for!"

He turned back to the fortress and made a big sign of the cross in the air in front of the strongly barred gates. Immediately Kieran heard the grating sound of the bolts flying back and the wide castle gates swung open. King Brude's men grovelled on the ground as Columba strode confidently inside, followed by his brother monks and the young servant.

"What magic is this that opens the doors of my castle without a man's hand touching them?" growled a huge, wild figure, as he came towards them.

"No magic," declared Columba, "but the power of the risen Christ, who wants all people to know him. He has sent me so that you and all your followers may have the gift of eternal life."

King Brude was awestruck by the miracle. He listened to Columba with reverence and soon he and all his followers were baptised. As Kieran marched behind the monks on the long walk home from Inverness to their tiny, windswept home, he marvelled at the power of God seen in this amazing man.

Kieran had seen many pagan Scotsmen converted in the short time since he'd been sent from Ireland to help at the abbey Columba had founded on the island of Iona. But this was the first time he had experienced the monk performing a miracle. It was not to be the last.

Columba was a tall, fine-looking man, with luminous grey eyes that shone with purpose. But his behaviour was strangely mixed. He drove the other monks and their servants with a power that sometimes scared them all. He had a foul temper, but he could also be very kind, especially to children and animals. He had always been good to Kieran.

Once, one of the monks had caught a well-known local thief in the act of stealing a seal. The monks kept a supply of seals trapped in one of the island's rocky inlets, as they were vital to them for food and fuel. Not only had Columba pardoned the thief, but he had sent him home with a sheep to console him for not getting the seal!

"We must keep the poor man from temptation," said Columba firmly.

Very early one morning Kieran was told to put supplies into one of the coracles, as they were going on another missionary expedition. He packed the small round boat with everything they needed and wondered if they were heading for the island of Lismore. He'd heard Columba and another monk, Moluag, arguing about it last night. Moluag felt it was his turn to claim a new place in the name of the Lord.

Kieran saw Columba striding down the rocky path to the shore and yawned. Columba must have won the argument – as usual. Surely it didn't matter who did it as long as it was done! If Moluag had won, Kieran wouldn't have had to get up hours before dawn.

They paddled out into the darkness in silence. The cold mist wrapped itself around Kieran like a blanket of ice and he shivered inside his rough tunic. Sunrise over the mainland of Scotland was a spectacular sight when it came at last, and they both looked back to admire its beauty. Not far behind them was another coracle, paddling swiftly in the same direction.

"It's Brother Moluag!" said Kieran in surprise.

Moluag and his servant were paddling briskly,

ignoring Columba completely.

"He's trying to beat me to it!" muttered Columba in amazement. "He's trying to get to Lismore first and claim it for himself to evangelise!"

Kieran stopped paddling, so astounded was he at this strange battle of wills.

"Paddle, boy!" roared Columba.

Kieran set to work eagerly and soon they had drawn farther ahead of the others. Lismore was in sight now, but he was tired by the effort. Moluag's servant was strong and much bigger than Kieran. The second coracle began to gain on them again. They were neck and neck as the two small boats neared the shoreline. Columba began to climb over the side.

Suddenly Moluag leapt up in his boat, his axe in his hand. Kieran nearly dropped his paddle in terror. Moluag was a monk. Surely he wasn't going to kill both of them just so he could get his own way!

With a roar Moluag lifted the axe high in the air. He brought it down on his own little finger with a resounding crack! Before Columba could clamber out of the boat, Moluag picked up the finger and threw it onto the sandy shore ahead of them.

"With my own flesh and blood I take possession of this island, and I bless it in the name of the Lord!" he shouted.

Moluag and the youth leapt out of the boat and splashed their way onto the sands.

Columba roared with anger. He refused to land on Lismore at all after that, not even for a bite of breakfast. Kieran was cold, wet and hungry as they set off back to Iona, with Columba muttering violently.

Not long after this strange event Kieran and Columba were returning from another missionary expedition inland. As they reached the loch of the River Ness they saw a group of people carrying the body of a man from the loch.

"Go and see what's happened," ordered Columba.

Kieran raced off and was soon back with the news.

"A huge water monster in the loch tried to eat that man!" he panted breathlessly. "It's bitten his legs right off! They pulled his corpse out with hooks and they're going to bury him now. Some people down there are converts and they want you to bless him first. But most of them are Picts and they say no!"

Columba and Kieran walked down to the group of Scotsmen.

"We must cross this loch," said Columba immediately. "I see a boat on the other side. Will one of you men swim over and get it for me?"

The people gasped with shock.

"Are you mad, monk?" exclaimed one. "Can you not see that there's a monster in yon loch? Who in their right mind would swim out there to certain death!"

Kieran shuddered with fear.

"Please, God, don't let Columba make me go!" he prayed silently.

But a man called Lugneus was already plunging into the water. The crowd watched in tense silence as he headed off, swimming strongly for the far shore.

Suddenly a huge head on a long dark neck broke the surface of the loch. The water monster opened its gigantic jaws and lunged towards Lugneus. Kieran screamed and so did many of the others. The rest sank to the ground and hid their eyes in terror.

Columba raised his hand and drew the shape of the cross in the air.

"In the name of God I command you!" he said. "Go no further! Do not touch the man! Go back at once!"

The water monster drew back as though pulled by ropes and retreated quickly to the depths of the loch. Lugneus brought the boat back, unharmed, and everyone was astonished. The pagan Picts who were present were overcome by the greatness of the miracle they had seen. They all began praising the Christian God and begging to hear more about him.

Kieran couldn't wait to get back to the abbey and tell the others what he had seen. Moluag may have claimed an island but Columba, with the help of God, had conquered a monster!

Fact file 1 file 2

- St Columba was born in Donegal, Ireland in AD 521.

- He was given the name Colum, meaning dove. The Latin version is Columba.

- Legend tells that before he was born an angel told his mother that she would bear a son of great beauty who would be remembered among the Lord's prophets.

- He was descended from the Irish kings and was in line for the throne, but gave it up to become a priest.

- He was chosen by St Finnian to be one of his Twelve Apostles of Ireland. Colum spent the first forty years of his life in Ireland, where he was known for working miracles. He was a poet and also loved fine books and manuscripts.

- He was very kind, especially to animals and children, but also had a very violent temper.

- Columba secretly copied a book belonging to his old master, Finbar. When discovered, Colum was not allowed to keep the copy. In anger, Colum roused his own clan to attack and, during the battle, 3,000 men died.

- He was very sorry afterwards and as a penance agreed to leave his beloved Ireland and become a missionary amongst the pagan tribes of Scotland. There he was told to win as many souls for Christ as had been lost in battle.

Fact ⟨ Fact file 2

✎ In AD 563 Columba sailed with twelve followers to found a monastery on the Scottish island of Iona. From there they travelled all over Scotland.

✎ Columba worked constantly in manual labour, prayer, reading and writing and made a large number of copies of the Gospels. For over 30 years he slept on the hard ground with a stone pillow, which is still preserved in Iona.

✎ It took Columba his whole life to conquer his pride and violent temper, but he did it with God's help. He became a gentle old man, meek and lowly in heart.

✎ St Columba is said to have foreseen the bloodshed in Ulster. He said, "My Irish people are to me a cause of sorrow, since in time to come they will wage war on one another, will injure, hate and wickedly slay, will shed innocent blood."

✎ St Adamnan, ninth abbot of Iona, described the account of Columba conquering the Loch Ness monster in AD 690.

✎ Columba died on Iona in AD 597 and is buried there.

✎ His feast is kept in Scotland and Ireland on 9 June, the day he died.

Chapter Three

Cartwheels and thundersticks

Virginia USA, December 1607

"Twelve cartwheels in a row!" said Pocahontas breathlessly, as she sank down beside her friends.

"One for each year of your age!" said her friend, Bright Eyes. "I think you can turn cartwheels better than any of us!"

"Better even than the boys," agreed Running Deer. "But we'll get in trouble if we don't have any pots made when the women come back. Come and help, Pocahontas!"

The girls were coiling long rolls of clay into pots but, as usual, Pocahontas would rather play. She took up a lump of clay and reluctantly started work.

"Did you hear about the white men my uncle saw by the coast?" she said excitedly. "They came from big floating islands in the bay. He said he saw them point a big stick at a bird. There was a noise like thunder and it fell out of the sky!"

"A thunderstick!" exclaimed Running Deer. "What sort of magic is that?"

"Strong magic!" said Pocahontas. "He thinks they are coming to fight the Powhatan tribes and steal our land!"

"I wish I was a boy!" declared Bright Eyes. "I would find these men with their thundersticks and kill them all before I'd let them on our hunting ground!"

"I wouldn't want to be a man and go to war," said Running Deer with a shudder. "I like working with the women. What about you, Pocahontas? What would you like to be?"

"I'd like to be an eagle," said Pocahontas dreamily. "I'd fly away across the sea and find out what it's like in other lands far away."

The other girls laughed. Pocahontas had always been a dreamer.

"Why do my father and the other chiefs think of nothing but war?" said Pocahontas crossly. "These men might just be coming to trade. I'd love to meet people from other places. I wouldn't kill them, I'd talk to them!"

Before long Pocahontas had her wish. The settlers had put Captain John Smith in charge of trading with the local Indians. This was successful for a while. John was very fond of children and always gave a small toy to any youngster brave enough to approach him.

But the Indians and the new settlers had already had several battles, with men dying on both sides. John Smith had been captured and was being marched to a meeting of the chiefs. The atmosphere in the Indian village was tense. Everyone was on edge, wondering if the arrival of John Smith and the other settlers would lead to a major war. The Indians were brave fighters, but they were very frightened of the magic thundersticks that could kill from a long distance. Would there be armies of settlers waiting to ambush them if they dealt harshly with Captain Smith?

Pocahontas helped prepare her father's ceremonial bed, laying mats and animal furs across the wide raised platform. She heaped up piles of soft deerskin pillows embroidered with pearls and then ran to her parents.

"Can I help you now?" she whispered to her mother, who was painting Chief Powhatan's head and shoulders with red dye.

"Put the pot of bear grease to warm by the fire," said her mother.

Pocahontas pushed the clay pot of precious fat into the embers at the side of the smoky fire in the middle of the longhouse and watched carefully as it softened. Then she took it to her mother, who rubbed it into Chief Powhatan's body until it glistened. Many chains of pearls were hung around his neck and a huge cloak of raccoon skins was flung around his shoulders. Then he put on his feather headdress.

"You're my favourite daughter, Pocahontas," said the chief, when he was ready to receive the other chiefs. "You shall sit at my feet when the prisoner comes."

Pocahontas was pleased. She was longing to see this strange white person. She had heard that he was a kind man who had already learnt a little of her language. Perhaps he would talk to her and answer all her questions about life across the seas.

The lesser chiefs arrived at the longhouse, looking just as fierce and war-like as her father. Pocahontas began to worry as she heard them talk.

"We must kill the men with the magic thundersticks before they kill us!" said one chief angrily.

"They have other magic too," added Powhatan's brother. "When we first captured the prisoner he said that if we took a piece of his paper back to his friends at the fort they would do certain things for us. Three of my men took the paper and it was exactly as he said. The magic paper must have talked to them and told them what to do! They could have magic even more evil! We must destroy them all!"

"I thought most of them had sailed away in their gigantic canoes," said Chief Powhatan, looking splendid on his luxurious bed.

"Many did," said his son, Nantaquas. "But those who are left are exploring our lands all the time, just like the prisoner I brought in. They want to take the land from us!"

"They have been here many moons already," said another. "They've cleared land on our hunting grounds and now they are ploughing it!"

"Bring the prisoner in!" commanded Chief Powhatan.

Several braves leapt to their feet and dragged the prisoner in. Pocahontas had expected a huge monster, but he was a rather short man. She couldn't see much of his skin, but what she could see was very pale indeed. He had a great bushy beard such as Pocahontas had never seen before in her life!

His clothes were very strange and covered him from neck to toes. He wore baggy trousers the colour of pine trees and long boots that met the trousers above his knees. His arms were covered in the same material as the trousers and over his chest was some strange hard stuff that glinted in the light of the fire.

"Serve him!" commanded Chief Powhatan, with a glance at Pocahontas.

She leapt to her feet and ran to get a wooden bowl of water for him to wash his hands. As she waited beside him with a bunch of feathers to dry his hands Captain John Smith caught her eye and, seeing she was only a child, smiled at her. Then she brought him water to drink, and a large platter of succulent roast venison.

"Thank you!" he said, in her own language.

He grabbed the haunch of meat in both hands and ate as if he hadn't had a good meal in weeks. Chief Powhatan waited politely until the man had eaten before he questioned him.

"Why are you here on our land?" he asked.

"We are trying to find a sea route to the East – to the Indies," said John Smith. "You know – the salt water beyond the mountains."

"It's a lie!" yelled Nantaquas. "They want to steal our sacred hunting grounds!"

"Kill him!" came a cry from one of the other chiefs.

Soon it rose to a roar.

"Kill him! Kill him! Kill him!"

Chief Powhatan got to his feet and picked up a massive club studded with sharp bears' teeth. Two of the men grabbed John Smith and threw him face down onto the ground, holding his arms behind his back. The chief raised the club above the white man's head and got ready to strike the fatal blow. Without thinking, Pocahontas leapt to her feet and flung herself across the man's body, shielding it with her own.

"Stand back!" roared her brother, Nantaquas. "The man must die!"

"No!" said Pocahontas. "I claim this man for my own!"

There was a gasp from the assembled tribe, but Chief Powhatan lowered his club.

"Pocahontas has that right," he reminded them. "All women of our tribe may claim a prisoner as their own if they are willing to look after him. The man is hers!"

For two days Pocahontas hardly left John Smith's side, except to do cartwheels of joy. This always made him laugh uproariously and he and the little Indian princess soon became firm friends. She taught him more of her language and even learnt a few words of English.

Then John Smith was taken to another of Chief Powhatan's longhouses, deep in the forest. He was left alone but he could still hear the Indians chanting just outside. He wondered if they were going to kill him after all. Then Chief Powhatan appeared, closely followed by a crowd of warriors. They were all painted black and John Smith feared the worst. But he was soon pleasantly surprised.

"Pocahontas has saved you and you could be like a son to me," said Chief Powhatan. "Would you like that?"

"Certainly," said John Smith. "I would be most honoured."

"That's settled then," said the chief. "You can go back to your fort and fetch me two of those magic thundersticks and a grindstone. Then we will be friends!"

So began a time of peace that lasted as long as

John Smith remained in Virginia. Pocahontas visited him frequently over the next few years, bringing presents of food and furs. She always asked him lots of questions about life in England.

"I wish I could go there and see it all one day," she said wistfully. "I'd love to see the royal court and all the people in their strange clothes."

"Keep on dreaming, little princess," laughed John Smith. "I'm sure your dream will come true one day!"

Years passed. Pocahontas got married and became a Christian. Eventually she did go to England and met the king and queen.

Fact file 1 \ file 2

- ✎ Matoaka ('little snow feather') was born in 1595. Native Americans believed harm would come to a person if outsiders learned their tribal name. So they nicknamed her Pocahontas, meaning 'playful little girl'.

- ✎ She was the eldest daughter of Chief Powhatan, who ruled 32 Indian tribes in Virginia.

- ✎ In April 1607 white settlers came from England to found Jamestown, Virginia.

- ✎ In December 1607 Pocahontas saved Captain John Smith from being executed.

- ✎ In January 1609, Pocahontas again saved John Smith's life and that of the other settlers, when she warned them of her father's plans to kill them.

Fact / Fact file 2

- In October 1609, John Smith was badly injured by a gunpowder explosion and was forced to return to England. Pocahontas was told that her friend Smith was dead. Peace between settlers and Indians was over.

- In 1612 Pocahontas was captured by the English captain Samuel Argyll and used as a hostage in his dealings with her father.

- In April 1614 she became a Christian. She was baptised an Anglican and given the name Rebecca.

- In the same month, she married John Rolfe, who had taught her to love God and read the Bible.

- Their marriage began a period of peace among the Powhatan Indians and the people of Jamestown. It became known as the 'Peace of Pocahontas'.

- In 1615 their son, Thomas Rolfe was born.

- They travelled to England in 1616 and had a happy year there. Pocahontas was known as 'Lady Rebecca, the Indian Princess'. Banquets and dances were given in her honour, and famous artists painted her portrait. She attended court and met King James I and Queen Charlotte.

- She was also joyfully reunited with John Smith, whom she'd thought was dead.

- They set sail to return to America in 1617, but Pocahontas became very ill and they returned to England.

- Pocahontas died in Gravesend, Essex, in March 1617, aged 21.

Chapter Four

Pilgrim daughter

Mayflower, Plymouth, England, 1620

Mrs Brewster shouted at her sons, "Love! Wrestling! Get away from the side of the ship or you'll fall in! I doubt if anyone would bother to rescue such troublesome boys. You'd be paddling round Plymouth Harbour for the rest of your days, living off the fish you could catch with your toes!"

Mrs Brewster sighed as her young friend, Mary hauled the boys backwards to the safety of the deck. Mary just smiled. She enjoyed looking after the two mischievous boys. Love was nine and Wrestling only six and they were always in trouble. The expedition was just fun to them. But Mary Chilton was nearly thirteen. She knew how Mrs Brewster felt.

"It's hard to be leaving family and friends behind," she said sadly. "We'll probably never see them again."

"But it's no longer safe to stay in England," said Mrs Brewster, with another sigh.

"Father thought we'd be safe when he took us to Holland," said Mary. "But it was just as bad there. People threw stones at us when we went outside!"

The king had commanded that everyone worship in the Church of England. But the Pilgrims wanted to worship God in their own way. So now they were heading for a strange new land, where they could be free.

"Is it true that there'll be wild savages called Indians?" asked Wrestling. "Love said they kill everyone they see – and eat them! Is it true, Mother?"

"People have travelled to the New World for a hundred years," replied his mother, "but few English sailors have been there. We don't know if the tales of wild Indians are true. So we'll face our troubles as they come and rely on the good Lord to watch over us. There's no point in worrying about Indians when we still have this great ocean to cross! Now, let's all go below and sort out our bedding."

As the three children staggered across the slippery deck, they knew that they were setting out on the biggest adventure of their lives. But they had no idea how hard it was going to be.

One hundred and thirty-two people were packed into the small wooden ship. They had pigs, goats and chickens, all kept in small boats lashed to the deck. The hold was packed with goods too. There were books, furniture, clothes and linen. There were pots, knives and tools. There was armour and weapons to fight the Indians. There was dried and salted food and cheeses. There were even 139 pairs of boots and shoes!

Mary was travelling with her parents. The Brewster and Chilton families shared the space below decks with dozens of other people. Anyone taller than Love couldn't stand upright in the crowded, dark quarters. It was too dangerous to use candles. They might make the wooden ship catch fire.

The weather was often stormy and the ship was tossed by the huge waves. The people were thrown about and were constantly seasick.

"Let's go up on deck and get away from this disgusting smell!" said Mary. "Don't worry, Mrs Brewster, I'll look after the boys."

Love and Wrestling eagerly started up the ladder. But as Mary struggled to open the hatch the wind roared along the decks. It brought with it a freezing surge of sea water, which poured through the hatch, drenching Mary and the boys. It was not safe for them to go on deck.

Even below decks they couldn't escape the weather. The icy rain poured through the cracks in the deck onto the shivering passengers below. Their lumpy mattresses and blankets were always damp and mildewed. There was no toilet, just a bucket that could be emptied overboard – when it wasn't too rough. It was a hard, horrifying journey.

Then, after more than two months at sea, there was a shout from one of the sailors, "Land ho!" They were in sight of America at last. The Pilgrims fell to their knees and thanked God. The Mayflower arrived at Cape Cod in November 1620. But the Pilgrims stayed aboard the ship at first.

This time brought great sadness for Mary and her mother. Her father died on 18 December 1620, while the Mayflower was docked in Provincetown Harbour. James Chilton was one of the oldest of the Mayflower passengers, but that didn't make it any easier for his family.

The leaders aboard the Mayflower decided not to stay at Cape Cod and continued down the coast. They made their own government with fair and equal laws, but they still had to choose somewhere to build their homes. Soon the snows would come. Some of the men set off in a small boat to explore the coast. Love longed to go with them.

"You can't come with us, lad," said Captain Miles Standish, the soldier in charge of the exploration. "You've got no armour and besides, you're only nine years old. Even my musket is taller than you!"

When the explorers returned with tales of Indians and a fine place for a settlement the Pilgrims were both excited and scared. Mary and the two Brewster boys managed to get into the first boat taking John Alden, the Pilgrim leader and his followers ashore.

"I'm going to be the first Pilgrim to set foot on the new land," boasted Love. "I'm going to try and jump off before Master Alden!"

"Me too!" declared Wrestling.

Mary said nothing. But inwardly she thought, Why should it always be the men and the boys who do things first?

There was great excitement aboard the launch as it bumped against the coastal rock. The Pilgrims had decided to name their new colony Plymouth, after the English city they had left. The big rock that the first settlers stepped onto was to be known ever after as Plymouth Rock.

John Alden started towards the front of the boat. But Mary lifted up her long skirts and raced ahead of him. Before anyone could stop her she leapt out and stood proudly on the flat rock. Mary Chilton was the first white female to set foot on Plymouth Rock.

The sailors had agreed to let the Pilgrims live on the ship until their settlement was built but it was to be a long hard winter. There were animals in the woods but they didn't know how to trap them. The ground was frozen so they couldn't plant their seeds. They found they hadn't brought the right sort of hooks to catch the teeming fish. The Pilgrims were very hungry.

It took three weeks to build one big house, where they could all live together at first. Later they started to build a series of one-room wooden houses, with thatched roofs. They had a terrible winter. It was so cold and damp and they had so little food that more than half of the 102 Pilgrims got sick and died. One of these was Mary's mother.

"What will become of me now, with both Mother and Father gone?" sobbed Mary.

"You're already like one of our family," said Mrs Brewster, comforting her. "I know the boys love you like a sister. Of course you'll stay with us now."

Two other teenage girls, Elizabeth and Priscilla, who also lost their families, soon joined Mary at the Brewsters. The three soon became inseparable.

The Pilgrims often saw campfires in the distance and they knew these belonged to Indians, so they were always scared of being attacked. Then one day Love came racing into the big house.

"Come quickly!" he yelled. "There's an Indian outside our house!"

Sure enough, there was an Indian, carrying a bow

and arrows. Master Brewster ran for the musket. But the Indian held up his hand.

"Welcome!" he said.

"He speaks English!" said Mrs Brewster in astonishment.

The Indian's name was Samoset. The next time he came he brought with him another Indian called Squanto, who spoke even better English. Squanto came to live with the Pilgrims. He taught them to hunt and fish and sow corn. Without him, the remaining Pilgrims almost certainly would have died.

But many of the Pilgrims retained their fear and distrust of Indians.

One day Elinore Billington came rushing into the main house.

"Has anyone seen my son John?" she cried.

Mary went out to help look for him. A high wooden wall surrounded the small settlement. A few minutes search proved that John really had disappeared. They eventually gave up hope for the boy, convinced that he must be dead, probably killed by the Indians.

But a month later two Indians brought him back. They had found him and looked after him. John's rescue did much to reassure the Pilgrims of the good intentions of the Indians. Squanto acted as interpreter and a peace treaty was arranged that lasted until Mary was an old woman.

Squanto's instructions had paid off well. By next autumn the Pilgrims were able to harvest enough food to see them through the coming winter. The corn grew well. Fish, meat and fowl were salted and stored. Fruit and vegetables were dried for the winter. A holiday was declared. The Pilgrims and the Indians would feast together.

Mary spent hours turning the spit on which a huge deer roasted. It was hot work but the delicious smell more than made up for that. She felt happy listening to the excited chatter of Mrs Brewster and the other women as they prepared the feast. There was great thanksgiving to God for his goodness and that so many had survived.

At last, the deer was roasted and the food prepared.

"Let's give thanks to God and eat!" said Mary contentedly.

Fact file 1 file 2

- ✎ The Pilgrims left England on 6 September, 1620, to find a land where they could worship God in their own way.

- ✎ They sailed from Plymouth in a 90-foot ship called the Mayflower.

- ✎ It took them 66 days to cross the Atlantic Ocean, to a place on the east coast of America, which they also named Plymouth.

- ✎ The famous painting, 'The Landing of the Pilgrims', by Henry Bacon, shows Mary being the first female to step out of the launch onto Plymouth Rock.

Fact / Fact file 2

✎ Mary Chilton was born in England in 1608. When she was 16 she married John Winslow, who came to Plymouth on the Fortune in 1621. They had 10 children and eventually moved to Boston, where John became a successful merchant and ship owner. Mary died there in 1679.

✎ During their first hard winter more than half the Pilgrims died. But all the girls and 10 of the 13 boys survived.

✎ The Pilgrims weren't the first people to live in Plymouth, Massachusetts. A visiting English sailor had kidnapped an Indian called Squanto. He took him to England and to Spain, but after many years Squanto managed to return home.

✎ When Squanto got back he found his whole tribe had died of plague. He went to live with another Indian tribe. But when the Pilgrims arrived he returned and stayed with them for the rest of his life. He used his survival skills to save them from starvation.

✎ To celebrate and give thanks, the Pilgrims and the Indians had a three-day holiday. They ran races, played games, ate and drank and thanked God for their blessings.

✎ Nearly 400 years later, Thanksgiving is still celebrated enthusiastically in North America every autumn.

Chapter Five

Johnny Appleseed

Ohio, USA, 1812

"Johnny Appleseed's coming!" yelled Paul joyfully. "Can we go and meet him, Ma?"

There were still many unfriendly Indians in the territory and the children were not allowed out of sight alone. But Ma knew that the Indians respected and admired the young man who lived so close to nature. The children would be safe enough if Johnny Appleseed was near.

"Go on then," she laughed. "But remember, it's dinner time soon."

The boys raced down the hill. A strange figure strode towards them. He was a small wiry man, with long, black hair tied back behind his ears. He had a wispy black beard and carried a huge pack.

Sally finished pulling the long green leaves from the last piece of corn and wiped her hands on her apron.

"Come on, Martha; it's Johnny Appleseed!"

Martha stood still, her mouth hanging open with surprise. She'd never seen such a weird figure in her life.

"Who on earth is that funny-looking man?" she gasped. "And whatever is he wearing? It looks like an old flour sack! And what's that on his head?"

Sally laughed.

"That's his cooking pot," she answered. "He carries it like that when there's no room for it in his pack. He says it's a good way of keeping his Bible dry when it rains!"

"But who is he? And what's so important that he has to fill his pack with it and carry his Bible and his cooking pot on his head?" asked Martha, incredulously.

"Apple seeds!" said Sally happily. "He's already planted apples right across Pennsylvania and Ohio, and he's always heading west to plant more. And he tells the best stories in the world! Come on!"

Sally and Martha soon reached the spot where Johnny and the boys were sitting on the grass under a spreading tree.

"This is Martha!" said Sally. "She's Billy's sister. Their family's just come from back east and built a cabin nearby, but they may have to go back soon."

The man's face and neck were bronzed and lined by wind and sun, although he was obviously still young. But it was his eyes that astounded Martha. They were piercingly brilliant, dark eyes that seemed to be able to see right inside her. But they were such kind eyes that the young girl immediately felt comfortable with the strange-looking, barefoot man.

"Hello, my dear," said Johnny. "Something tells me that moving back east won't make you happy. Why are you going?"

"My mother's been so ill she nearly died," answered Martha. "The doctor's bills are so big that we may have to sell the cabin to pay them. Then we'll only have enough money to go back east. But Pa hates the city! He's always wanted to live out here in the wilds – and so have we!"

"I too love the wilderness," he said, with a dreamy look in his eyes. "It's my home as I follow the sun to the west. I love the woods, where the birds sing and the squirrels play, and the spring breezes waft the sweet smell of blossom."

"Tell Martha and Billy some of your stories, Johnny!" interrupted Paul eagerly.

"I've heard about you!" said Billy. "Is it true that you once fought a bear with your bare hands?"

"No, that never happened," said Johnny with a deep laugh. "Although once I found a bear and her cubs asleep in a hollow log that I'd just built my fire against."

"Wow!" said Billy. "Did you roast them and eat them?"

"All creatures of nature are made by God, just as we are, and I look on them all as my brothers," said Johnny firmly. "I would never harm a living thing. No, I put out the fire so that it should not disturb them and curled up to sleep in the snow nearby."

"Weren't you afraid they'd wake up and attack you?" asked Billy, his eyes wide. "Just like all the wild Indians you meet?"

"I've never been attacked by Indians, nor by anything else!" said Johnny. "I live in harmony with all people and all creatures."

"So you don't wrestle Indians – or bears," said Billy dolefully.

"Very few of those stories you've heard about me are true, I'm afraid," said Johnny with a smile. "What I really like is reading the Bible and sharing it with others. I like putting seeds into the soil and watching buds turn to bushes and trees. I've been a poor man in the eyes of men, but I feel God has showered me with many blessings in this world."

"Why don't you wear any boots?" asked Martha. "Don't your feet freeze in the snow and ice?"

"No," said Johnny. "My best travelling is done during winter months when the cold has settled in and my feet are bare. The icy earth quickens my step even faster!"

"Aren't you afraid that your toes will freeze right off?" asked Billy.

"No, never," said Johnny. "I still have all six I started out with!"

Both Martha and Billy looked at his bare feet incredulously, counting the toes. It wasn't until Johnny, Sally and Paul started to laugh that Martha realised that it was a joke.

"Dinner time!" called Ma.

Martha's parents came over for dinner too, and the family stayed for hours. Johnny told enough exciting adventure stories from the Bible, of lion wrestling, seas being parted, and a giant fish swallowing a man that even Billy was well satisfied.

Martha was sad to leave Johnny and his stories behind when the family set out for home. But she'd seen him give her father a piece of paper and couldn't wait to find out what it was.

"It's the answer to our prayers!" declared her mother.

"It's a map, Martha," said her father. "In spite of his ragged looks, our new friend is not a poor man. But he doesn't keep his money in banks. He buries it here and there in the forest."

"Like a pirate!" exclaimed Billy.

"Yes," agreed his father. "This map will lead me to a place not too far away where he has buried some money. He says it will be enough to pay off all our bills and even set us up for the coming winter. Johnny Appleseed is a friend indeed!"

Martha longed to see the odd, kindly man again. But she never dreamed that their next meeting would occur in such strange circumstances. It was 1812 and America was at war with Britain. Many Indians had joined the British side. They weren't interested in the reasons for the war; they just wanted to seek revenge for injustices done to their people by the American settlers.

These hostile Indians attacked throughout Ohio territory, but they left Johnny Appleseed alone. Large bands of them were rampaging throughout the territory. They destroyed everything they found, burning homes and crops. They even killed the women and children. Johnny Appleseed roamed around the country, warning settlers of danger.

On one occasion, he learned that a band of Indians was attacking the town of Mansfield. He ran twenty-six miles through the forest to get help for the settlers. As he ran, he tried to warn other settlers along the path of the danger by blowing on an old powder horn. Help reached the town within a day, and the settlers were spared, thanks to Johnny's bravery.

Martha and her family were sleeping soundly one moonlit night, a few months after they'd first met Johnny Appleseed. Suddenly they heard a loud knocking at their cabin door and a voice they recognised.

"The spirit of the Lord is upon me. He has appointed me to blow the trumpet in the wilderness and sound an alarm in the forests. Look out, for the heathen tribes are nearing your house and a devouring flame is following them!"

"Put your warmest clothes on!" shouted their father. "Get some food and all the firearms and knives we possess!"

"Go right over to your friends' house," said Johnny. "They have a blockhouse and you'll be safe from the Indians there."

"Won't you stay and rest?" said their mother. "Or at least take some food?"

"I must go on and warn the rest of the families," said Johnny. "I just pray that this wretched war will be over soon and I can go back to planting apple seeds. For a land without apple trees is no land at all!"

As Martha followed her family to the safety of blockhouse she could still hear the voice of Johnny Appleseed singing as he tramped through the woods.

Oh the Lord is good to me
And so I thank the Lord
For giving me the things I need
The sun and the rain and the appleseed
Oh the Lord is good to me!

For every seed I sow
An apple tree will grow
And there will be apples there
Enough for the whole wide world to share
The Lord is good to me!

Fact file 1 \file 2

- John Chapman was born on 26 September 1774, at Leominster, Massachusetts.

- He became known as Johnny Appleseed because he planted apple seeds wherever he went.

- Johnny looked for soil that was fertile, and then he would plant seeds. When the trees were partly grown, he returned to tend them and repair the fences he had built to keep out animals.

- He created apple orchards in the wildernesses of the American Midwest, spanning an area of 100,000 square miles. Some of these trees are still bearing fruit after 200 years.

- Johnny loved the wilderness. The longer he lived and the farther he travelled, the deeper became his faith in God and his love for all living things.

- Johnny Appleseed was a committed Christian and always carried his Bible. People loved to hear him read it and talk about the love of God.

- In 40 years he walked, mostly barefoot, 10,000 miles. He lived on herbs, wild fruit, berries, nuts and cornmeal mush.

- He also sowed the seeds of medicinal herbs wherever he went, as there were few doctors around in pioneer times.

- Johnny learned many Indian languages and was respected by the Indians who believed he was touched by the Great Spirit. He became a peacemaker between Indians and settlers, as he had compassion for the views and needs of both cultures.

Fact   Fact file 2

✎ Although dressed in rags, Johnny Appleseed was not poor. He eventually owned about 1,200 acres of orchards. He used the money for charity and to further his work, rather than for his personal comfort.

✎ Although he was a brave military hero in the war of 1812, he refused to kill anything – even animals for food.

✎ He would often rescue aged or ill-treated horses and pay some farmer to care for them.

✎ He never stayed long anywhere, but everywhere he left three blessings – love, faith and the apple tree.

✎ John Chapman died from pneumonia at the age of 71, on 18 March 1845. It was the first time in his life that he'd been ill! The last words that he spoke were from the Sermon on the Mount.

Chapter Six

Black Moses

Maryland, USA, 1826

"This white baby's got a pretty bed, Mammy. Look at all those frills!"

"It's called a cradle, Harriet," replied her mother. "See how it rocks. That's going to be your job. The Mistress says six years old is plenty old enough to be working for your keep."

"The baby's not as pretty as the cradle, Mammy," answered Harriet. "It's all wrinkled and ugly! How come it's bright red? I thought it was a white baby."

"Hush, Harriet!" said her mother, looking around anxiously. "Don't talk like that about Master Baby! You don't know the ways of the big house yet. You could get us both into big trouble!"

"Master Baby!" spluttered Harriet. "Don't tell me I've got to call that scrawny little red thing 'Master'! He's just a tiny baby and I'm much bigger than he is!"

The woman knelt down and grasped her young daughter firmly by the shoulders.

"Listen to me, Harriet! That little baby is white, like the Mistress and the Master. You are black. That makes him your Master, whatever his size. We are nothing but slaves and you're old enough to understand exactly what that means now. If you forget that for a single minute then you'll remember it for the rest of your life!"

"What do you mean, Mammy?" asked Harriet. "How can I remember what I forgot?"

"If you do the least little thing wrong, Harriet, the white folks will beat you. If they get out of bed in a bad mood, they will beat you, even if you've done nothing wrong! You're a slave, Harriet. You have no rights. You must just obey, no matter what. That's what you must remember."

"But I don't want to be a slave, Mammy. I don't want to rock the baby's cradle. I want to go out and play!"

"You are what you are, Harriet. You're black. You're a slave. Nothing can ever change that. Now, I've got to get back to the kitchen, or I'll be in trouble too. If Master Baby starts to whimper, then you rock the cradle and get him back to sleep."

"Shall I pick him up and cuddle him if he cries, Mammy? That always quiets the babies at home."

"Don't touch him, Harriet! The Mistress said she didn't want your little black hands touching her precious baby! Just rock him."

As the door closed behind her mother, Harriet was filled with fear. She didn't want to be left alone. What if the baby woke up? She sat down by the cradle and looked at him.

The baby couldn't do anything but yell and suck and soil his pants. Harriet could talk and sing, run and dance, make cat's cradles and catch little fish in the river. How could he be better than her just because he was white?

Then the sleeping baby screwed up its face and began to whimper. Harriet started to rock the cradle, making soothing noises. But it did no good. Soon the baby began to howl. Harriet rocked harder. Then the baby began to scream. Mammy had said just to rock the cradle, so Harriet rocked harder still. She rocked so hard that the baby rolled straight out of the cradle and onto the floor!

Harriet reached to pick him up. Then she remembered her mother's warning. She mustn't pick him up with her own black hands! She looked around desperately for something to use to pick up the howling baby. She must get him back into the cradle and quiet before anyone heard him.

Harriet ran and got a small shovel from the fireplace. She had managed to scoop the baby up with the shovel and was trying desperately to tip him back into the cradle when the Mistress came in.

Harriet was taken outside and given a violent whipping. As the terrible blows rained down on her, little Harriet made herself a promise. She would always be black. But one day, somehow, she would not be a slave. It was to be the first of many awful whippings, often for no reason. Harriet was so badly whipped, and so often, that her back and neck remained scarred for the rest of her life.

She was put to work in the fields like an animal. She had been angry about the injustice of slavery since her first whipping. One day, when she was about 13, the owner was whipping another of the young slaves. Harriet ran to try and help him. The owner threw a huge stone at the boy. The boy dodged the stone and it hit Harriet on the head. She was so badly injured that she nearly died. For the rest of her life Harriet suffered pain and disablement from that blow on the head.

By the time she was in her twenties, Harriet was married to John Tubman, a free African American. But Harriet was still a slave. One day she staggered into the tiny cabin she shared with John. She had terrible news.

"The Master's going to sell me and a lot of the others! He's sending us down to Georgia in a chain gang! You've got to help me, John!"

"How can I help you, Harriet? I haven't got the money to buy you and that's the only way you could be saved."

"It's not the only way! I've got to escape to the north where I can be free! Help me, John!"

"You must be mad, girl!" replied her husband. "You know what they'd do to me if I helped you to escape! I can't risk my life – even for you!"

"But John, you know that I'd die long before I ever got to Georgia! I couldn't survive a chain gang! You must help me escape!"

"Never! Forget it, Harriet. You were born a slave and you'll die a slave! I'm not going to help you escape. And if you try it, I'll report you to your Master. He'd probably beat you to death when he caught you! Now, forget all this nonsense and get me my supper!"

Harriet had always known her husband was a coward, but she never thought he might betray her. She burned with rage, but said no more about escape. She cooked supper for him and watched until he was snoozing by the fire. Then she swiftly put a little food in a bag, wrapped her shawl around her shoulders and ran away.

She knew she wouldn't get far by herself so she went to the house of a white Quaker woman she'd heard about. Quakers think slavery, violence and killing is wrong. They believe what it says in the Bible, that all men are equal in the sight of God. The kind Quaker woman kept Harriet hidden while her white master searched for her. He offered a huge reward for Harriet's capture, but the woman stuck fast to her beliefs and kept Harriet hidden until it was safe for her to move on.

Then she had the girl transported to another safe house further north. Harriet was very frightened. She knew she would be horribly tortured if she was captured. But she remembered that promise she had made to herself when she was six years old. She knew she had to be free.

Harriet moved from one safe house to the next, usually in the dead of night. Slowly she made her way up north to freedom along the secret escape route, which they called the Underground Railroad, even though there were no trains involved. Early one morning, in 1849, she crossed into the state of Pennsylvania, in the north of the USA, where slavery was not allowed. Harriet Tubman was free at last.

Although Harriet was free, the rest of her family were still slaves. When she heard that her sister was going to be sold, she decided to risk everything to try to save her. She went back down south, rescued her sister and led her to freedom along the secret escape route.

That was the first of many journeys made as a 'conductor' on the Underground Railroad. Each journey was more dangerous than the last, as the slave owners were determined to catch her. Harriet had to wear many different disguises to hide from them.

There was a reward of $40,000 offered for Harriet's capture. That was worth a huge fortune in those days. Many people would be tempted to give her away to the slave owners. But this didn't stop Harriet. She too had a strong belief in God, which gave her courage. During the next twelve years Harriet led more than 300 slaves to freedom. She was like Moses in the Bible, leading his people from slavery in Egypt.

Sometimes Harriet's "passengers" got frightened, and tried to change their minds about escaping. The chance for other slaves to find freedom would be destroyed if anyone discovered the Underground Railroad, so it was too dangerous to let anybody return. Harriet was a strong character. If her passengers ever got so frightened they wanted to return, she would point her gun at them and say, "Live north or die here." She knew they would thank her for it in the end.

Once Harriet used a real railroad to make an escape. Her parents were too old and frail to hide and walk the hundreds of miles of the escape route, as the other slaves did. Using disguises, she made a daring rescue of her parents from slavery and brought them north on a train.

Harriet Tubman was proud to say, "On my Underground Railroad, I never run my train off the track and I never lost a passenger".

✎ Slaves are people who are owned by their masters. Slavery has existed since ancient times. Slaves could be worked, starved, beaten, married off or sold away from their families, as their owner chose.

✎ Most of the slaves who worked on the plantations in the USA came from Africa. Fifteen million Africans were brought to America to work as slaves between 1500 and 1865. They were kidnapped or sold by their African owners.

✎ Slavery was legal in the southern states until the end of the American Civil War, which was fought to end it.

✎ When they were sold, slaves were made to walk to their new plantation, sometimes hundreds of miles away. They were chained together around the ankles and sometimes around their necks too. This is why it is called a chain gang. They were whipped to keep them moving. Many couldn't keep up and died along the way.

✎ Harriet is called 'Black Moses' because she led her people to freedom, just like Moses did in the Bible.

✎ During the American Civil War (1861–1865) Harriet worked as a spy and a scout for the northern Union army, often working in enemy territory.

✎ She has been honoured in many ways. During World War II a liberty ship was named after her. A postage stamp with her picture was issued in 1978.

Fact / Fact file 2

✎ With the pension from her war work, Harriet Tubman opened a home for black people who were too old to support themselves. She worked for social justice until she died in 1913, aged 93.

✎ There are still slaves in parts of the world today, including many children.

Chapter Seven

Shipwreck!

Longstone Lighthouse, Farne Islands,
Northumberland, 7 September 1838

"You go up to bed, Father. I'll put everything to dry by the fire," I said.

I was thankful that our four-hour ordeal was over. My father and I had been working since midnight, clearing our belongings from the rocky courtyard that surrounded our lighthouse home. A fierce storm was raging and the coming high tide would wash everything away. We had to save our tools, rabbit hutches, fishing gear, baskets of fruit and vegetables. We kept many useful things outside, because there was no room for them inside the lighthouse.

The wind had pushed and buffeted me. It kept blowing my long petticoats up over my head so that I feared I'd blow away like a balloon! All the time the rain lashed down from above, and from every side the furious waves sprayed us with icy salt water.

It felt good to be safe and dry again. Mother was taking the last watch of the night. She was up at the top of the lighthouse, tending the lantern. In about two hours it would be dawn, and hopefully light enough for the lantern to be put out.

I hung up the wet clothes and boots to dry, then climbed the winding stairs. I've always loved my tiny round room at the top of the lighthouse, with its small circular window. I feel safe and secure up there, so far above the fury of the sea. I love the seashells and birds' eggs that I've used to decorate my room.

Although I've grown up with storms, and am used to their noise and fury, I was glad to be safely indoors again. Our lighthouse is on a rock just a few feet above the sea, which can be a very scary place in a storm. I hate to admit it, but I'm really frightened of the power of the sea. If you'd seen as many wrecks and people drowned as I have, you would be too. I'm glad I'm not a lifeboat man like my younger brother, Brooks. I hope he's not out tonight. Surely no boat could go out in seas like these!

I went to the window to reassure myself that the waves were too high for anyone to risk launching a lifeboat tonight. Far below, the dark sea raged and roared, the waves as high as I'd ever seen them. In the light from the big lantern I could see massive walls of white spray hurtling against the rocks of the Hardcar reef. These were the nearest rocks, only three hundred yards away.

Shocked and amazed, I dropped my candle on the floor. Out on the Hardcar reef was a ship – or at least part of a ship. It was the remains of a large paddle steamer, smashed onto the dangerous rocks by the storm.

"Shipwreck!" I yelled, as I raced to wake my father. "There's a wreck out on the Hardcar reef!"

We ran to the top of the lighthouse, where

Mother was dozing by the huge lantern. Father grabbed his big telescope and tried to scan the wreck for signs of life. But it was too dark to see anything more than the dim shape of the wreck, like a ghost ship in the distance. The next two hours were desperate ones for us all. We didn't know if there were any survivors on the wreck. If there were, would the seas calm down enough for us to attempt a rescue?

Then dawn brought the grim sight of the broken masts of the ghost ship. The dim light also showed huddled figures on the black rocks, surrounded by raging seas. My father caught my eye and I nodded, even though my heart was thudding with fear. We'd have to try and rescue the survivors, even if it meant almost certain death for ourselves. Without a word we raced down to get out the boat.

"You can't go out in those waves, you'll be drowned in minutes!" wailed Mother, as she stumbled down the winding staircase after us.

"We must!" I said. "There are lots of people out there. We are their only hope!"

Still Mother implored us not to go.

"No, Grace! You know it takes three strong men to row the coble even in a calm sea. How can one man and a small lass like you manage in seas like these? The waves are twenty feet high!"

She wept as she ran out to steady the boat for us as we got in. She was convinced we would drown. I felt much the same way, but I knew I would never forgive myself if we didn't try.

"Wait and pray, Thomasin," said Father, who believed, as we all do, that the good Lord watches over us. "Prayer is the only thing that can help us now."

Although it was dawn, the storm had blackened the sky. The lashing rain blinded us, so it was hard to see enough of the treacherous rocks to steer clear of them without going out too far into the open seas. One moment the icy waves towered above us like huge grey sea monsters. Then we were lifted so high on the waves it was like hanging over a gigantic cliff, looking down into a dark, bottomless pit.

The wreck was only three hundred yards away, but we had to row more than a mile around the rocks to reach it without going to certain death on the reefs. As I pulled on the heavy oars I felt as if my arms were being ripped out of their sockets from the force of the heavy seas. I thought my wrists would snap, trying to match the strong strokes of my father. If I couldn't, the little coble would just go round in circles until it sank. So I prayed hard, and tried to imagine that my wrists were made of iron, to will them to haul on those oars.

The ship looks like a huge dying animal, I thought, as we neared the looming wreck. Sounds like one too! I could hear the ominous creaking it made, even above the howl of the furious winds. If it fell off the rocks and into the raging waters we would all be sucked down with it, into the cruel, freezing sea.

The people were clinging desperately to the black rocks, constantly drenched with spray, as wave after icy wave cascaded over them. I saw that one of them was a young woman. The people shouted and screamed and started to scrabble over the rocks, desperate to reach the small boat first. Father knew there would not be room for them all. He'd have to leave the boat and try to reason with the survivors.

"Row back and forth!" he yelled, as he passed his oar to me. "You must keep the coble off the rocks!"

Alone in the boat, I was more terrified than I'd ever been in my life. I committed my actions to God as prayer, for I knew there would be no time for words, or even thoughts. The sea tried to tear the heavy oars from my hands as I rowed backwards and forwards. The lashing rain and freezing spray blinded me so I never knew how I kept the boat off the treacherous rocks. I felt that my back would break and almost welcomed the icy hand of the sea to draw me in and end my pain. But the thought of the survivors, especially that poor woman, kept me going.

At last Father had selected the first boatload and waved me nearer. I rowed in as close as I dared and he carried out the wailing woman.

"Let me stay with my children!" the woman pleaded. "They need me!"

But Father shook his head at me and I knew the children were dead. Three sailors carried another injured man into the boat. Then the dangerous journey back to the lighthouse began.

Even with the sailors rowing too it took all our strength to get the small boat, now heavily laden, back to the lighthouse. I had never been so pleased to set my feet upon that slippery grey rock. As I helped the weeping woman out of the boat, Mother ran out and led her to safety. The rest of us carried the injured man up to the lighthouse, then I turned back to the boat for another hazardous journey to collect the other survivors. But Father stopped me.

"No, Grace," he said. "God has answered our prayers. The sailors from the wreck will row back with me to fetch the others. I reckon the three of them can just about match the strength of a young lass like you." He smiled proudly, despite the dangerous situation. "Of course, you're not just any young lass. You're a lighthouse keeper's daughter."

Fact file 1 \ file 2

- Grace Darling, aged 22, was the seventh of nine children, the only one still living with her parents in a lighthouse off the coast of Northumberland.

- Longstone lighthouse was built in 1826. It was a hundred feet high with three bedrooms and a big kitchen/living room at the bottom. At the top was the big lantern, which shone all night to warn ships to steer clear of the treacherous rocks.

- Grace's father, William Darling, was the lighthouse keeper. It was his job to polish the reflectors that threw the light farther out to sea. He also had to measure and record the height of the tides every hour.

- There were no electric lighthouses then and William had to keep the lantern filled with oil and the wick trimmed so it would burn brightly. One of the family always kept watch by the lantern to make sure it didn't go out.

- The Forfarshire was a big paddle ship, run by steam. It was travelling from Hull to Dundee when its engines stopped working during the storm. It was blown onto the Big Hardcar rock, where it broke in two. The back half was swept away, drowning nearly fifty people. But twelve people were left on the front half, which was caught on the rock. A man and two children died, but the other nine were saved.

Fact | Fact file 2

✎ The brave rescue soon made them famous. Photography was almost unknown, so artists came to the lighthouse to paint portraits of Grace and her father. William Darling complained that they had posed for eleven artists in a fortnight and he no longer had time to do his job!

✎ So many people wrote to Grace to ask for her autograph and a lock of her hair that she would have been bald if she'd let them all have one! She received many medals and presents, including £50 from Queen Victoria.

✎ Although a small young woman, Grace was strong and free from illness when she lived on her lighthouse out at sea. But four years later she took a trip to the mainland to visit her sister and caught a bad chill. In those days people didn't believe in the benefits of fresh air, especially during illness. Grace was kept indoors and never regained her health. She died some months later, aged only twenty-six.

Chapter Eight

In search of the missing link

Antarctica, 1911

"The Emperor penguin could be the missing link between birds and reptiles!" said Bill excitedly.

"Are you sure about that, Bill?" asked one of his fellow explorers.

"Of course I'm not sure," Bill Wilson said patiently. "A scientist is never sure until he has the facts in front of him that prove his theory. That's why we need to go to Cape Crozier and collect some eggs with embryos in them!"

The members of Captain Scott's second Antarctic expedition were gathered in the large hut they had built about four months ago at Cape Evans. It was certainly better than a tent. The three layers of insulated floorboards kept out some of the cold from the bone-chilling ice beneath them. There were even three glass windows, through which the explorers could see the darkness of the polar winter.

"The Emperor penguin egg holds vital clues to the evolution of birds," continued Bill. "We think the primitive Emperor embryo will prove that there is a link between reptilian scales and birds' feathers."

"All we've got to do is go and fetch some," said Cherry with a smile.

Apsley Cherry-Garrard was the youngest member of the polar expedition and could always be relied on to be cheerful.

"I think you're right," said Captain Scott, the expedition's leader. "Wilson must go, of course, as chief scientist. Harry Bowers and Cherry-Garrard can go with him."

Bowers was pleased. He was nearly as mad about birds as Bill and his nickname was 'Birdie'. Cherry had been Bill's friend since long before the polar expedition and would gladly have gone anywhere with him.

"It will be a 105 kilometre journey, so you'll need to be well prepared," said Captain Scott. "This winter travel is a new and bold venture, but I'm sure I've chosen the right men to attempt it."

They were ready to leave by 27 June. The three men set off, pulling the laden sledges themselves. Their equipment was very bulky and heavy. Their sleeping bags were made from reindeer fur. These were warm, as long as they were dry. But that didn't last for long. At night the men would sweat, which produced a puddle beneath them. By morning the bags were frozen solid, as were boots and mittens. At best their sleeping bags and clothes were wet and cold, at worst, frozen stiff and icy.

The hard labour of dragging the heavy sledges through the soft snow and across uneven ridges of solid ice exhausted the men. The raging blizzards and dark conditions of the polar winter meant that often they could see nothing, not even their partners.

"Polar exploration must be the cleanest and most isolated way of having a bad time which has ever been devised!" said Cherry ruefully, as they tumbled into their tent after a day's hard slog across the bumpy polar ice.

"You're right!" said Bill, as he lay where he had fallen. He was so exhausted and so cold there was literally nothing else that he could do. He wrinkled his nose and started to spit and blow.

"I hate the way the reindeer skin hairs get in your mouth and nose and you're too frozen to lift a hand to get them out!" he said. Then he gave a wry laugh. "There's a fascination about it all, but it can't be considered comfort!"

As they made their way over the Ross Ice Shelf the temperature dropped to –77 degrees. They had to negotiate dangerous pressure ridges and crevasses. The last twenty kilometres were undertaken in almost complete darkness, which made it even more dangerous.

It took 18 days for the men to get to the Knoll, near the penguin rookery just above Cape Crozier. They were so shattered all they wanted to do was lie down and rest. But the weather was getting even worse and that would have meant certain death.

"At least there's a good crop of rocks here," gasped Birdie. "A stone shelter will protect us from the wind.

They staggered back and forth with their arms laden with rocks. They slowly built a stone igloo-shaped shelter. The wind raged and roared about them and at times it was only the weight of the rocks they were carrying that kept them from being blown away.

"Help me get the tarpaulin secured over the top," Bill yelled. "We can't stay out here any longer!"

Several times the sheet of canvas nearly took flight, but at last they were able to fasten it down with more heavy stones. They pushed the sleds up against the igloo, threw some of their belongings inside and collapsed on top of them. The blizzard screamed and roared about them for ten long days. After the first three days they couldn't even get out of their sodden sleeping bags.

"There's not much food left," said Birdie gloomily. "Nor much fuel either. How much longer do you think we can last?"

"We must pray for the storm to let up long enough for us to collect the eggs we came for," said Bill. "We can also kill some of the penguins. We'll eat their flesh and use penguin oil for fuel."

"Bill's right," said Cherry. "I'm sure we'll make it."

After ten long, bitterly cold days the wind died down enough for them to venture outside. They found themselves on an outlying cone of the mountain, about 13,000 feet above the sea. Below them lay the emperor penguin rookery on the bay ice. The Ross Sea was completely frozen over, a plain of firm white ice stretching into the distance.

"This must be the windiest place on the face of the earth," muttered Birdie.

The sky was black and threatening and before long it began to snow again. The weary men headed back to their shelter. Next morning a gale was blowing again, making it impossible for them to get out at all. The blizzard continued all day and night. They lay in their stiff sleeping bags and thought about their loved ones at home. Would they ever see them again?

"Praise the Lord, it's clear!" said Bill next morning, as he cautiously poked his head out of the stone shelter.

The men lost no time in heading for the edge of the cliff overlooking the rookery. They could see that the migration of the Emperor penguins had started.

"Let's go, chaps!" said Cherry enthusiastically.

They were surprised to find only about a hundred birds left at the rookery. First they caught and killed three birds for food. Bill carefully skinned them, so he could get them stuffed at home. They put six eggs gingerly into their pockets and began the difficult trek back up the 900-foot cliff. The journey back to the shelter was extremely hazardous, with several near-death plunges into some of the many crevasses. But Bill had only one thing in mind.

"Are the eggs all right?" he asked anxiously, when they made it to the top at last.

They turned out their pockets with numb fingers clumsy with cold. Bill was dismayed to find that three of the precious eggs had been smashed. But they quickly realised that this would be the least of their troubles. A gale was blowing and the climb had totally exhausted the three men. They could barely stumble into the shelter of their stone igloo before they collapsed.

That night a hurricane swept across the Knoll as they shivered inside their stone shelter and wondered if it would be their tomb. The men tried to keep each other cheerful, even amidst the desperate cold and gnawing hunger. But Cherry was in horrible pain from toothache. Bill looked in his mouth in the flicker of the penguin oil lamp and declared, "You poor chap! This terrible cold has cracked all your teeth!"

The noise of the hurricane was terrifying, but Bill had to take a fleeting look outside when they felt the sleds against the stone wall lift in the wind. He was just in time to see their one and only tent ripped off the sled. It billowed like a sail at sea then took off like a giant bird into the lashing blizzard.

The men were gloomy as they realised what this would mean. They could not make the long journey back to Cape Evans without the shelter of a tent. Bill was not the only man who prayed for a miracle that night. It seemed at first that miracles were not coming their way. An even worse noise filled their tiny shelter.

"It's the roof!" yelled Birdie. "We're losing the roof!"

The wind had got under their canvas roof and shredded it like tissue paper. They huddled together against one of the stone walls until the storm passed. In the initial calm, all they could do was write in their diaries, knowing they would probably never be read. Cherry wrote, "We on this journey are already beginning to think of death as a friend."

They went outside and Birdie and Cherry wearily began to dig in the snow for their belongings. Bill walked out to take a last look at the Emperor penguins. The other men were astounded to hear a roar of delight from about 400 metres away.

"It's a miracle! It's the tent!"

It really was a miracle, as the tent was undamaged. On 25 July they set off to return to

Scott's base. Starvation and exhaustion nearly killed them on the way, but six days later they staggered into the hut at Cape Evans.

"They look like dead men walking!" exclaimed Captain Scott.

Their friends were astonished and delighted to see them. They set about cutting off their frozen clothes, which were like chunks of solid armour. Cherry's sleeping bag weighed eight kilos when he left. The 36-day journey added another 11 kilos of caked ice to it!

They were given bread and jam and cocoa, and showered with questions. On the gramophone a scratched record of George Robey was playing. This started the three weary men laughing so much that in their weak state they found it difficult to stop.

"Well, we've survived the worst journey in the world," said Cherry.

"For the sake of science and three Emperor penguin eggs!" said Bill, with a contented smile.

They were helped into warm blanket bags, and Cherry managed to keep awake just long enough to think, "Paradise must feel something like this."

Fact file 1 \ file 2

- ✎ Edward Adrian Wilson (known as 'Bill') was a zoologist, artist, doctor, Antarctic explorer and committed Christian.

- ✎ He was born in Cheltenham, the son of a doctor. As a boy he was fascinated by the natural world and began drawing at an early age.

- ✎ He studied natural sciences at Cambridge University, and later studied medicine.

Fact / Fact file 2

- As a young man he got pulmonary tuberculosis after spending too many chilly nights birdwatching and starving himself so he could give money to beggars or to buy books. He spent two years recovering in sanatoriums in Norway and Switzerland.

- He went on Scott's Antarctic expeditions in 1902 and 1911.

- He was an excellent artist and made many drawings and paintings on his expeditions, even though it was so cold that he could take his mittens off for only seconds at a time.

- On 27th June 1911, Wilson, Bowers and Cherry-Garrard set off on a 105 km journey to reach Cape Crozier Emperor penguin colony to collect eggs. Wilson wanted to see if they were the missing link between reptiles and birds. (They weren't!)

- The trip was made on foot, hauling sledges in the darkness of the polar winter night. In some of the worst storms ever recorded, the temperatures reached -77°F. They nearly died, but eventually returned safely.

- Wilson later reached the South Pole with Scott, only to find that the Norwegians had got there first.

- In April 1912 Wilson, Scott, Evans, Oates and Bowers died on their way back from the South Pole.

- Cherry-Garrard survived and died in 1959.

- Wilson felt God's presence in everything he saw and did, and believed whatever happened was in his plan. Having no fear of death, it's not surprising that his last words, written minutes before his death, were: "All is well".

Chapter Nine

The small storyteller

China, 1944

> WANTED!
> ONE HUNDRED DOLLARS REWARD
> The Imperial Japanese army will pay $100
> for information leading to the capture of
> the Small Woman, known as Ai-weh-deh.

"A hundred dollars!" said Gladys in amazement. "Who'd have thought I was worth a fortune!" She handed the 'Wanted' poster back to her friend.

"You must escape quickly!" he said. "The Japanese know that you've been spying for the Chinese army. They're determined to kill you!"

"You're right," said Gladys. "I must get back and make sure my children are safe!"

China was at war with Japan, and many of the local people had already been killed. Gladys crept through the deserted city. Suddenly she heard a party of soldiers returning. She must get past them somehow and escape. As she ran she could hear the soldiers shouting. They had seen her! Bullets whizzed around her ears as she headed for a field where she could hide. Suddenly she felt a great thwack in her back and fell flat on her face. She'd been shot.

Bullets were still thudding into the dust around her. They were using her body for target practice! Gladys quickly unfastened her thick padded coat and wriggled out of it, leaving it lying on the ground. She had fallen onto her large Bible. Using this like a sledge under her stomach she wormed her way forward until the tall grain hid her.

Then she burrowed through the corn until she reached the other side of the field. She could still hear the bullets flying. There must be hundreds of holes in her coat by now. Thankfully, the thick coat had saved her from serious injury. The bullet had just grazed her shoulder blade. She knew she would have to hide until it was dark before she could risk going back home.

Gladys loved China so much! She had been glad to help by going into enemy-occupied territory to get information to help the Chinese. That was why she was in danger now. As she lay curled up in the field, she thought about the events that had brought her to China.

She had been a young servant in England and longed to become a missionary in China. So she went to Bible College for three months. But she was never very good at exams and it had not been a success. Gladys Aylward was only as big as a ten-year-old, but she was very determined. She knew God wanted her to go to China, so she saved her money until she had enough for the cheapest fare.

She'd had many adventures over the years. She'd learnt Chinese and was already famous for her storytelling. Everywhere she travelled she told the eager people exciting Bible stories.

As time went by she had collected unwanted

children. There was Sualan, a slave girl, and a dirty little boy known as Dusty Heap. One child was called 'Sixpence', because that was how much Gladys had paid for her. She eventually adopted five of the children as her own.

But as the war continued there were very many children whose parents had been killed. Many were brought to Gladys because people knew she would love them and look after them. She cleaned them up, fed them and told them stories. They liked the story of Moses best. Soon she had nearly a hundred children to look after.

It was these children Gladys was thinking about as she lay shivering with cold. The New Life movement ran orphanages for abandoned children. She knew if she could get them to safety, then New Life would look after them. Otherwise the Japanese might kill them.

As soon as it was dark she started her perilous journey back to the children. She was determined to take them all to safety. The children were overjoyed to see her again and crowded round, begging for stories.

"I want you all to go to bed early," she said. "Tomorrow we are going on a long, long walk! Don't forget to bring your bowls and chopsticks with you."

The children cheered. What an adventure! Gladys knew she had no food or money for the journey. But she was sure that God would provide.

At dawn the children were ready to go. Although there were 30 bigger ones, over 70 were under nine years old and there was even one toddler. They raced about madly, even though Gladys told them to save their energy for the long walk ahead.

For the first few days things went fairly well. But it was very cold at night. They had no blankets so they all slept huddled together to keep warm. The bigger boys took turns to keep away the rats that swarmed everywhere at night.

They had been given some grain to make porridge, but after a few days it ran out. Their thin cloth shoes were worn through and their feet were cut and bleeding. Gladys prayed for God to provide once more. Two of the boys came running.

"Soldiers!" they shouted. "Take cover!"

The children immediately scrambled into the rocks and hid, as they had practised so many times. Japanese planes flew overhead, but no machine-gun bullets rained down. They had not been seen.

As the children came out from the rocks Gladys felt her heart leap with fear again. About fifty soldiers had also appeared from hiding. But a glance at their dirty uniforms reassured her.

"*Our* soldiers!" shrieked the children, leaping up and down with joy and relief. That night the children feasted on the supplies the soldiers willingly shared with them.

But from then onwards, each day was worse than the last. There was little to eat. The weary line of children left a darkened trail behind them, as the dust soaked up the blood from their cut feet. Gladys encouraged them onwards with stories and songs. She always carried several of the smaller ones, who cried and complained. But all of them kept on going.

On the twelfth day they were overjoyed to see the Yellow River. Crossing the wide river was their only route to freedom. But when they got to the river they found no people in sight and no boats.

"Can't you be like Moses and make the river part so we can walk through?" asked Sualan, remembering her favourite story.

"I am not Moses," said Gladys wearily.

"But God is still God," said Sualan.

"You are right, my child," said Gladys. "God will find some way for us to cross this river. Let's sing and pray until he shows us the way."

A Chinese soldier was amazed to hear the sound of children's voices in this deserted place. Was it a Japanese ambush? He investigated and found Gladys and the children beside the river. Gladys told him that they were refugees, trying to reach safety.

"Don't you realise that this will soon be a battlefield?" asked the soldier in amazement.

"All China is a battlefield," replied Gladys. "I must get these children to safety across the river."

"If the Japanese spot you they will sink the boat and you will all die anyway," he said.

"If you can get us a boat, then God will get us safely across," Gladys assured him.

The soldier had never heard anything like it. But it was too dangerous to leave a hundred children here. He whistled for a boat from across the river. Silently another soldier rowed a boat across. The children shivered from cold in the bottom of the small boat as it crossed the huge river. It took many journeys but eventually they were all safely across.

Once across the river they walked for a few miles to a village. Here the people were glad to share their food with the hungry children.

"Couldn't we stay here?" asked Dusty Heap. "My feet hurt so much and these people are kind. I'm sure they'll look after us. "

"The Japanese are coming," said Gladys firmly. "They'll be here before you know. We must get as far away as possible."

Even the young ones had heard that the Japanese would have no mercy. They made no more complaints as Gladys moved them on. They spent the night in the fields, then moved on to an old temple. Gladys had just settled the children down to sleep when the door crashed open and several burly policemen burst in.

"We want the woman who crossed the Yellow River!" they shouted.

Without another word they dragged Gladys off to the police station. The bewildered children trailed after them, rubbing the sleep from their eyes. They weren't going to let Ai-weh-deh out of their sight for a moment.

"You are charged with crossing the Yellow River without permission. Under the war conditions this is not allowed. What have you got to say in your defence?" they demanded.

Outside the police station the children waited impatiently. They banged on the windows with their fists and yelled, "Let her out! Let her out!"

"If you're going to arrest me, you'll have to arrest all my children too!" said Gladys. "There are a hundred of them and they take a lot of feeding! Surely you didn't expect us to stay there and wait to be killed?"

The police muttered amongst themselves. At last they decided that arresting Gladys would be too much trouble, so they released her. She managed to get all the children onto a goods train travelling away from the Japanese. They journeyed for about four days, until the train came to a bridge that had been blown up.

"We can't go any further by train," Gladys told the weary children.

"We've been travelling for more than three weeks already," sighed Sixpence. "We've all had so little to eat. Just look at those high mountains! How will we ever cross them?"

"We will because we must," said Gladys. "We've come this far. We can't stop now. It is no safer here, so we must go on until we reach freedom. Be brave, Sixpence, we can do it!"

They travelled very slowly now, their feet so sore that each step was agony. Everyone was exhausted, but Gladys and the bigger boys still managed to carry the little ones. It was bitterly cold up in the mountains. At night they huddled together in caves to keep from freezing. Along the way they begged food from the villages they passed. But there were so many of them that each meal was no more than a few mouthfuls. It was a ragged, thin band of children who eventually reached the plain on the other side of the mountains.

Gladys discovered a railway line and found that coal trains travelled along it in the direction they wanted to go. But there was still danger. The train passed close to Japanese positions.

"It's impossible! If they realise anyone is aboard, they'll machine-gun the train," people told her. "You won't be able to keep all those children quiet! You'll all be killed!"

But it was the only way to freedom. Gladys knew how deeply the exhausted little children slept at night. She settled them down to sleep near the railway. When they were sound asleep, Gladys and the older children made a human chain and passed the little ones along it, placing them carefully amongst the lumps of coal in the wagons. As the train started its perilous journey the children slept on. They didn't wake until dawn, when they were astounded to find that they all looked very different.

"You've turned black in the night, Ai-weh-deh!" they yelled. "We've all turned black. Isn't it funny!"

It was another week's walking before they reached the outskirts of Sian, the city they were headed for. The children were glad to settle down and rest while Gladys went on alone. But the gates of the walled city were closed.

"Go away, woman!" the guards yelled down to her. "The city is packed with refugees. There is no room for you. Go away!"

Had they endured nearly two months of danger and hardships just to be turned away? If she couldn't get into the city, how could she find the people who had promised to look after the children? She couldn't feed a hundred children for the rest of their lives! Gladys prayed once more before she began the weary walk back to the children.

But the leaders of the New Life movement had already found the big group of children. By the time Gladys arrived back, they had food cooking on a big campfire and the children were warm and well fed for the first time in weeks. They had arranged places in a big orphanage and school for every one of them. A few days later the children departed for their new home, already well fed and better clothed.

Gladys and her own five children waved them off. In many ways she was sad to see them go. But she knew she had succeeded in leading one hundred children to a better life. Now she was ready to go back to telling Bible stories and helping Chinese people through the war.

Fact file 1 \ file 2

- Gladys Aylward lived from 1904–1970.

- She was a London parlour maid who 'failed' theological college. They told her she too small and weak to survive life in China and not clever enough to learn the language.

- In 1932 Gladys went to China by train across Europe, Russia and Siberia, enduring freezing cold and hunger for a month. She had £2.09 for food.

- In China she worked at an inn for the men who ran mule trains. Muleteers stayed there because they loved stories. So Gladys learned the language by memorising Bible stories to tell to the muleteers at night.

Fact / Fact file 2

✎ In China the feet of girl babies used to be bent back and bandaged to make them tiny. This was very painful and made walking very difficult. Then a law was passed forbidding this and Gladys became a Foot Inspector, going around the country telling people to unbind their little girls' feet. As she travelled she told stories from the Bible. People were always pleased to see her.

✎ When Gladys became a naturalised Chinese in 1936 she took the name the Chinese had given her, Ai-weh-deh. It means 'the virtuous one'.

✎ During the war Gladys worked as a spy in Japanese occupied territory. The Japanese attacked a mission house she was working at and she was badly injured. After the trek Gladys became dangerously ill from the hardships she had endured and her injuries from the Japanese.

✎ When her five adopted children grew up she returned to England for a much needed operation. But she came back to her beloved China eight years later, where she became the head of an orphanage. She was reunited with many of the children she had rescued.

Chapter Ten

The secret room

Haarlem, Holland, 1944

"We have an old watch with an unusual face. Do you know anyone who would buy it?"

Corrie watched her father deal with the customer. Requests like these were common now that their Dutch city was overrun with Nazi soldiers. This was a watch shop and it had been in their family for over 100 years. She and her father, Caspar, were both watchmakers. But she knew that the man was not really a customer. Nor did he want to sell a watch.

He was part of the Resistance, a group of loyal Dutchmen who were secretly fighting the Germans. The Nazis wanted to exterminate all Jews. They captured them and sent them to concentration camps, where millions were eventually killed. Anyone who helped them would also be arrested and sent to these horrific camps.

His request was a secret code. Corrie and her father were also members of the Resistance, so they understood that the man was looking for a safe place for an old man who looked so Jewish that his identity could not be hidden.

As soon as the customer had left, Caspar came over to where Corrie was working.

"We'll have to house some of the Jews ourselves," he said. "Willem has no more room and we're running out of safe houses to hide them until they can escape. The Jews are God's chosen people and so much of our precious Bible comes from them. We must do more to help them."

Corrie's brother Willem was a minister who had been looking after Jews for a long time. He and his son Kik already had many more Jews than they could deal with.

"But, here, Father?" said Corrie incredulously. "Wouldn't that be too dangerous? We're only a hundred metres from Haarlem Police Station! Besides, how could we feed them? You know everyone needs a ration card to buy their food now!"

"If it is what God wants then he will provide a way," said Caspar simply.

Corrie ten Boom was well used to dealing with problems. Over the years the family had given homes to foster children and orphans. Their home had always been an 'open house' for anyone in need. This was one of the ways they showed their Christian faith. She herself had runs girls' clubs for nearly twenty years. Whenever Corrie had a problem she prayed about it.

The first obstacle was finding ration cards. As Corrie prayed, a man called Fred came to mind. His daughter had attended her clubs for years and now she remembered that Fred worked in the office where ration cards were issued. She visited him to ask if he could help.

"No way!" he said firmly. "I'd like to help, but it's just too dangerous!"

But a few days later he came into their shop. He had a black eye and bruised face.

"Whatever's happened to you, Fred?" asked Corrie, greatly concerned.

"We had a robbery at the office," replied Fred. "It was terrible! Some of the ration cards were stolen. I just wanted to leave my grandfather's old watch to see if you could mend it."

But as he handed Corrie the envelope containing the watch he gave her a big wink. Corrie took the envelope into their living room above the shop before she opened it. Inside was a pile of ration cards.

Soon after she went to a meeting of the Resistance. Everyone there was secretly helping the war effort. If an English plane was shot down they'd attempt to rescue the pilot. If they discovered that a train was taking ammunition to the Germans they'd blow it up. If Dutch Resistance workers were arrested they'd try to free them.

Corrie met an architect who offered to design a secret room. He was very pleased with the ten Boom's old house when he came to look at it.

"This is a perfect house for a secret room!" he said. "It's an odd shape with many nooks and crannies. But you need it as far away from the front door as possible, to give people more time to hide when someone comes."

Corrie's bedroom was at the top of the house and he chose that as the best place. He marked off a space 75 centimetres from the back wall.

"We'll make you a cupboard, which you must fill with linen," he said. "But keep the space underneath the bottom shelf clear. Here we'll make a sliding door to the secret room. We'll put a false wall next to it and put a big bookcase in front of that."

Afterwards, many of the shop's customers had tools and materials hidden in their bags and under their coats. They worked with silent speed to get the job done. When it was finished, the cupboard and false wall looked as old as the rest of the house. The architect came over to inspect the work.

"This is excellent!" he said. "They'll never find this room! Now it's up to you to train your guests to cover all traces of their existence when they hide in the secret room. If they've been eating with you – hide their dishes. If they've been sleeping in one of the bedrooms – turn the mattress over. Some otherwise perfect hiding places have been discovered because the Gestapo felt all the mattresses and found there were more warm beds than people!"

Corrie shuddered at the thought of the Gestapo, the cruel Nazi secret police, searching her house. But even that didn't put her off. She was certain her family was doing what God wanted. Her mother had died and Willem and her sister Nollie were both married, but Corrie's oldest sister Betsie still lived at home with them. Soon the first 'guest' arrived. Most of the time they were joined in the big house by six guests, who were either Jews or Resistance workers in hiding.

They put in an alarm buzzer, with buttons in the shop and in several of the rooms. They practised constantly, until they could get from anywhere in the house to the secret room in less than a minute. During the war the ten Boom family and their friends helped over 800 people to hide and escape in this way.

One day a policeman came into the shop. It was Rolf, one of the Resistance workers.

"The Gestapo are planning to raid one of our safe houses," he said quietly, as he showed her his watch. "Can you send one of the boys to warn them?"

"I'm sure I can manage to fix that for you," said Corrie.

The boys were Dutch teenagers who also wanted to help their country against the Nazis and often acted as messengers.

"I'll go!" said Jop. "My aunt lives in the same street. I'll ride over on my bike and visit her."

Kik came over to the house that evening, looking desperately worried.

"You're all in great danger!" he said. "When Jop arrived the Gestapo had already raided the house. They captured him and now they'll torture him to get the names of all his contacts. They're so cruel that it would be impossible for anyone to resist, let alone a young boy! You must stop hiding people!"

"But they have nowhere else to go!" said Betsie.

"We've got six people here now, Kik," said Corrie. "They must stay!"

Caspar nodded in agreement.

"Then you must be very careful," said Kik. "But even that may not be enough now!"

Corrie had flu when the buzzer went, one day in February 1944. The guests raced through her bedroom and crawled into the secret room. Corrie had just shut the door of the linen cupboard after them when the Gestapo crashed through her bedroom door and dragged her downstairs.

"Where are the Jews?" they yelled, hitting her over and over again. "Where is the secret room?"

Soon Corrie was covered with blood. When they couldn't get anything out of her they started on Betsie. Soon she too was bruised and bleeding. Throughout all this the Nazis searched the house, smashing cupboards and kicking open doors. But they didn't find the secret room.

"Take this whole family down to the police station and guard this house!" said the Gestapo officer. "If there are any Jews hiding in here, they'll starve to death!"

Corrie and her family were dragged off and put in prison. She was so ill that she was put in a cell by herself for four months. It was bitterly cold and there was no bed, just a filthy mattress on the floor and a thin blanket that some previous prisoner had been sick on. But someone smuggled in part of a Bible to her and this comforted Corrie.

One day she was even allowed a parcel from her sister Nollie. It contained a bright red towel, some biscuits and a needle and thread. Corrie was delighted. As she nibbled a biscuit she noticed that the address and stamp on the parcel were very crooked. That wasn't like her neat sister, Nollie!

She carefully peeled off the stamp. Underneath were written the words, "All the watches left in the cupboard are safe."

Corrie gasped with relief. This meant that all the prisoners trapped in the secret room had somehow been rescued and released. It made their imprisonment worthwhile. Their work had not been in vain. Corrie smiled as she thanked God.

Fact file 1 / file 2

- Corrie (short for Cornelia) ten Boom was born in Haarlem in Holland on 15 April 1892. The youngest child of Caspar and Cornelia ten Boom, she had a brother Willem and two sisters, Betsie and Nollie.

- Her father was a watchmaker. When Corrie grew up she became the first woman in Holland to qualify as a watchmaker.

- Corrie ran a club for the mentally handicapped as well as clubs for girls aged 12–18, from 1921 to 1940. They did gymnastics, music, walking and camping. Corrie also taught them that God loved them, and that they could always turn to him in prayer. The Nazis banned these clubs.

- On 10 May 1940 German forces invaded Holland. Soon after this, the ten Boom family began helping Jews to escape from the Germans. They hid many Jews and Resistance workers in a secret room in their house.

- On 28 February 1944 the family were arrested. Caspar was 84 and died ten days after his arrest.

- Corrie was taken to prison with Betsie and Willem. Willem was released, but died shortly after the war from an illness contracted in prison.

- In June 1944 Corrie and Betsie were moved to a labour camp.

- In September 1944 the sisters were moved to the horrific Ravensbruck concentration camp in Germany. Corrie gave Betsie and other needy prisoners vitamin drops each day. She only had a tiny bottle but, just like the widow's jar of oil in the Bible, the drops never ran out.

Fact / Fact file 2

✎ Betsie died there just before Christmas 1944.

✎ Corrie's nephew, Kik, died as a German prisoner of war during the last few months of the war.

✎ Corrie was released on 31 December 1944. Afterwards she learned that she had been released by mistake. A week later all the women of her age in the camp were killed.

✎ The Allies liberated Holland on 5 May 1945 and Germany surrendered on 8 May 1945.

✎ After the war Corrie worked for forgiveness and reconciliation between former enemies. She visited over 60 countries.

✎ In 1968 she was honoured by Israel for her work in aid of the Jewish people, by being invited to plant a tree in the Avenue of the Righteous Gentiles, near Jerusalem. Corrie was also honoured as a War Hero by the Queen of Holland.

✎ In 1975 *The Hiding Place*, a film of Corrie's life, was released.

✎ Corrie settled in California in 1977. She died on 15 April 1983, her 91st birthday.

If you've enjoyed this book, why not look out for other titles from Scripture Union? Such as Angels *by Kathy Lee.*

It's Christmas, and the residents of Westhaven are puzzled by the disappearance of valuable paintings from the museum. But Grace's friends and neighbours have worries of their own. As she tries to go 'the extra mile' for those around her, Grace discovers that being kind can be costly.

And what will happen if it gets dangerous?
Will there be an angel around to help?

Turn the page for an extract from this exciting book.

Chapter 1

Burglars

"Dad's late," said Mum as she dished out steaming heaps of pasta. "We'll have to start without him. Grace, would you call the others?"

At once our dog, Jerry, shot under the table. He always knows when it's mealtime, and he lies there hopefully, waiting for someone to drop a crumb or two. (One day, Mum dropped a whole dish full of rice pudding. Jerry has never forgotten it.)

Ben, my ever-hungry brother, was next to appear. He's almost thirteen, two years older than me. Strangers never believe we are related because Ben is tall and dark like Dad. I'm more like Mum – small with curly, fair hair.

I also have a sister, Hannah. She's fifteen and a bit of a pain. As usual, she was up in her room with loud music thumping away.

"Hannah!" I banged on her door.

"What?"

"Supper's ready. Hey, loud music can make you go deaf, did you know?"

"What?"

I gave up and went downstairs. Dad was just coming in from the cold November night.

"Sorry I'm so late," he said to Mum, "but you'll never guess the reason why."

"Traffic, I suppose," said Mum. "Anyway, you're here. Sit down and have a cup of tea."

"Not traffic," Dad said mysteriously. "Go on, kids, have a guess why I'm late."

"You had to finish a job," I said.

"You had a puncture," suggested Mum.

"You were abducted by aliens," said Ben.

"But they didn't want him," said Hannah, arriving on the scene. "They were looking for *intelligent* life on earth."

Dad ignored this. "Wrong. You're all wrong. I've been involved in a burglary!"

We all, even Hannah, stared, open-mouthed.

"Well, not actually involved," he admitted. "But I'm a suspect. I've had my fingerprints taken by the police."

"Why?" Mum gasped.

"They've had a break-in at Barcliff Hall."

Barcliff Hall was a big house a few miles from Westhaven. It was open to the public – I had been there once on a school trip. I remembered it as a gloomy place... dark old furniture, faded carpets, paintings of ugly people in old-fashioned clothes.

Dad had been working there for the last few weeks, helping to build a shop and café for visitors. This new part of the building hadn't yet been fitted with a proper alarm system. The police thought this was where the burglars had got in.

"They fingerprinted all of us," said Dad. "Everybody who works there. Tour guides, cleaners, gardeners – the lot."

"So they think it was an inside job?" Ben said. "But why?"

"Well, those paintings were all fixed up with burglar alarms. If anyone tried to steal them, the alarm should have gone off – but it didn't. So, either the thieves were very lucky, or they knew how to switch off the alarm."

Mum asked him what else had been stolen.

"Nothing else. Just the three paintings, but they're supposed to be worth a lot of money – over a hundred thousand pounds."

"Really?" I remembered the pictures I'd seen at Barcliff Hall. I wouldn't have given a hundred pounds for the whole collection – but a hundred thousand! Forget it.

"They don't seriously suspect you, do they, Dad?" I asked.

"Well, I hope not. I said to them, what about all the visitors to the Hall? Any of them could have been thieves spying on the place, checking on the alarm systems."

"Did *you* notice anyone suspicious?" I asked him.

Ben said, "What do you think a thief looks like then, Grace? Black mask, stripy jumper and a bag marked SWAG, like in a comic?"

"Of course not. I'm not stupid," I said, annoyed. "I just wondered if Dad had seen anyone... you know, hanging about. Looking for ways to get inside the building."

"Not me," said Dad. "Too busy working, I am."

"Come on, sit down, love," said Mum. "The food's getting cold."

We started to eat. But all through the meal, I was thinking about those burglars. Who were they? What did they look like? Could you tell a criminal by his face – or would he look just like an ordinary person?

I almost wished I could meet one of the thieves. It would be exciting, I thought. (Well, how was I to know? The only criminals I'd ever come across were harmless ones in books.)

Always be careful what you wish for. It just might come true.

———————

Taken from *Angels*, Kathy Lee (SU)

ISBN 1 85999 445 8

Why not look out for these other Snapshots titles?

Muddle is my Middle Name
Kay Kinnear

Lucy jumped back and her foot skidded. She thumped down, "Oooof!" straight on to a plate of buttered toast on the coffee table. "Oh, Mum, sorry!" Lucy stood up and twisted round to look at her buttery bottom.

Lucy had promised herself things were going to change. She was going to really, really concentrate on keeping out of trouble. She was going to Become Organised, so she could make her dream come true.

ISBN 1 85999 457 1

Lion Hunt
Ruth Kirtley

High time, short point at four.
Climb a lofty guardian;
What stops his roar?

The clues seem baffling. Will Ashley and Rachel be able to work them out in time? And will the clues lead them to something that will save the house from being taken over by the scheming Mr Doubleby?

For Ashley, too, there is much more to this than a hunt for hidden loot.

ISBN 1 85999 412 1

Flood Alert!
Kathy Lee

It was stupid, I know that now.
But there was no time to think.
Helpless as a bit of straw, I was
tossed and shaken and dragged
under water. I fought my way
up – then before I could snatch
a breath I went under again.

"Help!" I shouted.

"Don't bother," said Kerry.
"They won't hear."

I was sinking. I was going
down for the last time...

ISBN 1 85999 301 X

*You can buy these books at your local Christian
bookshop, or online at
www.scriptureunion.org.uk/publishing or call
Mail Order direct on 01908 856006.*